Parent's Introduction

We Both Read is the first series of books designed to invite parents and children to share the reading of a story by taking turns reading aloud. This "shared reading" innovation, which was developed in conjunction with early reading specialists, invites parents to read the more sophisticated text on the left-hand pages, while children are encouraged to read the right-hand pages, which have been written at one of three early reading levels.

Reading aloud is one of the most important activities parents can share with their child to assist their reading development. However, *We Both Read* goes beyond reading *to* a child and allows parents to share reading *with* a child. *We Both Read* is so powerful and effective because it combines two key elements in learning: "showing" (the parent reads) and "doing" (the child reads). The result is not only faster reading development for the child, but a much more enjoyable and enriching experience for both!

Most of the words used in the child's text should be familiar to them. Others can easily be sounded out. An occasional difficult word will be first introduced in the parent's text, distinguished with **bold lettering**. Pointing out these words, as you read them, will help familiarize them to your child. You may also find it helpful to read the entire book aloud yourself the first time, then invite your child to participate on the second reading. Also note that the parent's text is preceded by a "talking parent" icon: ⊖ ; and the child's text is preceded by a "talking child" icon: ⊙ .

We Both Read books is a fun, easy way to encourage and help your child to read — and a wonderful way to start your child off on a lifetime of reading enjoyment!

We Both Read: About Space

Images courtesy of NASA and NSSDC

We Both Read® is a registered trademark of Treasure Bay, Inc.

Published by Treasure Bay, Inc.
40 Sir Francis Drake Blvd.
San Anselmo, CA 94960 USA

PRINTED IN SINGAPORE

Hardcover ISBN: 1-891327-39-9
Paperback ISBN: 1-891327-40-2

05 06 07 08 09 / 10 9 8 7 6 5 4 3 2

**We Both Read® Books
Patent No. 5,957,693**

Visit us online at:
www.webothread.com

About Space

By Jana Carson

TREASURE BAY

Let's take a journey into space, where we will see wondrous sights and make incredible discoveries.

What is space? Space is the **universe**. The **universe** contains everything!

 Have you ever looked way up at the sky?
It seems to go on forever!
But what we see in our sky is only a very
tiny part of the **universe.**

All of the galaxies, planets, stars, meteors, asteroids, and even space stations are a part of the universe.

A galaxy is a large system of stars held together in a group by gravity. We live in a galaxy called the **Milky Way.** We are able to view many of the stars in our galaxy through the use of a telescope.

Long ago people could only look at the stars with their eyes.

The stars of the **Milky Way** looked like a white streak in the sky.

 Within a galaxy there may be many **solar systems.** A **solar system** is made up of a sun and everything that moves around it.

Our **solar system** exists within the Milky Way galaxy. It consists of nine planets and their moons, comets, asteroids, and other space objects that orbit or move in circles around the sun.

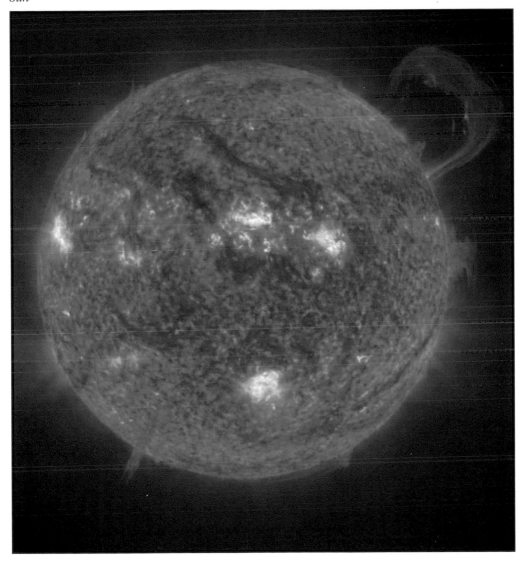

 There is a sun in the center of every **solar system.** A sun is really a star. Without our Sun, there could be no life in our solar system.

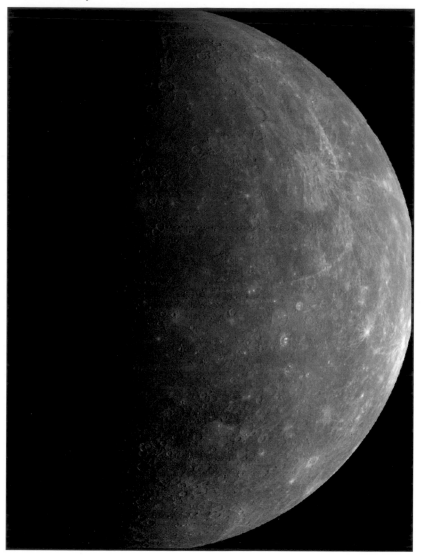

The planet we live on is called the Earth. Other planets in our solar system are **Mercury,** Venus, Mars, Jupiter, Saturn, Uranus, Neptune, and Pluto.

Mercury is the closet planet to our Sun. The temperature on the planet's surface is hot enough to melt a tin pan!

Mercury's densely cratered surface

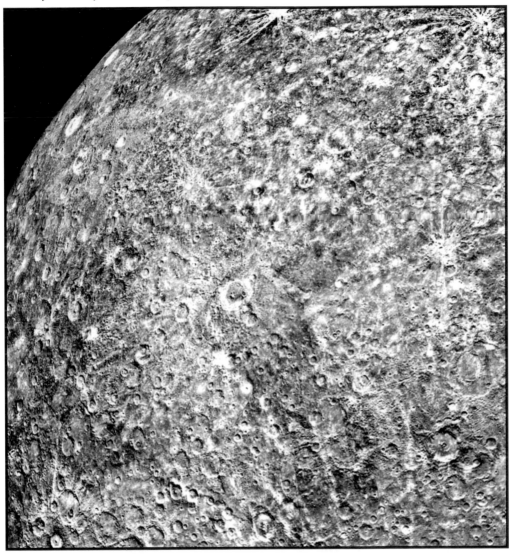

Ce **Mercury** is a small planet.

It is about the size of our Moon.

It is very, very hot on Mercury.

It is too hot for people to live there!

 **Venus** and Earth are similar in size and they both have mountains and valleys and plains. But there are no oceans or life of any kind on **Venus.**

Venus is covered with thick clouds. There are always huge thunderstorms in these clouds.

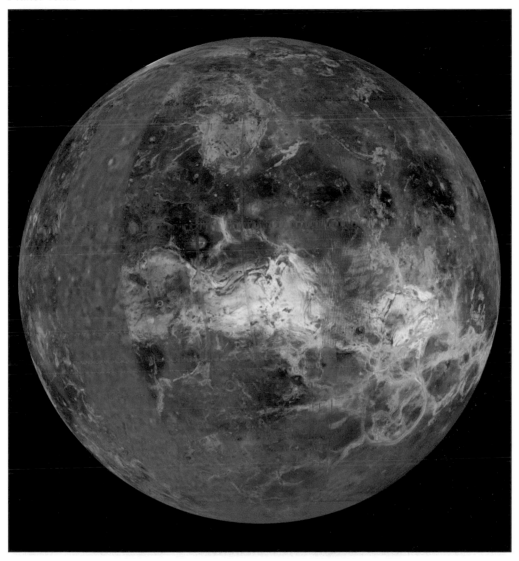

 Venus is called the Evening Star.
That's because it looks so bright in
our night sky.

Mars is called the red planet. **Space probes** were sent to **Mars** by the United States and other countries to collect information about the Martian soil and atmosphere. Through these experiments it was discovered that the dirt on **Mars** contains lots of iron. The iron is what gives **Mars** its reddish color.

 Some people hoped to find life on **Mars.**

But the **space probes** found no life there.

 **Jupiter** is the largest planet in our solar system. There are terrific lightning bolts and huge gas storms in **Jupiter's** atmosphere.

A large area of swirling gas called the Great Red Spot is believed to be a hurricane-like storm.

 **Jupiter** is very, very big!

All of the other planets in our solar

system could fit inside of **Jupiter.**

Saturn is a planet that spins rapidly on its axis—just like a spinning top. This rapid spinning causes something amazing to happen. The top and bottom of the planet flatten out!

It is believed that there are over 1000 rings surrounding **Saturn.** The rings are actually particles of ice and dust.

 **Saturn** has many moons.

Some of these moons are very big.

Saturn's largest moon is called Titan.

Some astronomers call **Neptune** and Uranus twin planets. That is because they are so much alike. They are both gas planets composed primarily of hydrogen and helium. They are both blue green in color, and they both have high winds that blow in their atmospheres.

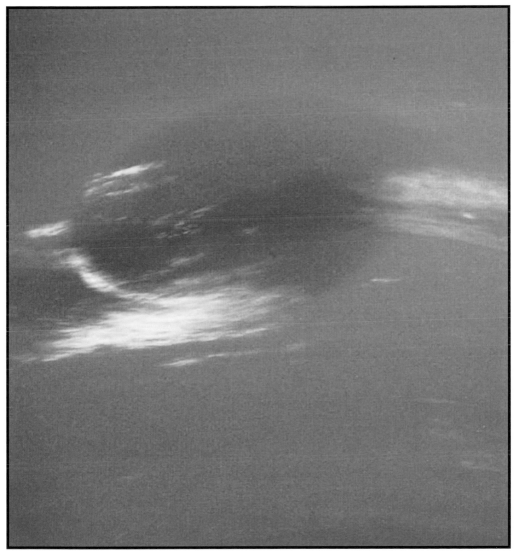

 Neptune has a large dark spot.

Neptune also has many rings around it.

Some rings are thick.

Some rings are thin.

Pluto is the farthest planet from the sun. It is sometimes called the frozen or ice planet.

Once every 248 Earth years, Pluto will cross over inside the orbit of Neptune. It will stay in Neptune's orbit for 20 years, and then it will go back to its original place.

Pluto and its moon

 **Pluto** is a very small planet.
It has only one small moon.
Pluto's moon is about half the
size of **Pluto.**

 **Earth** is our home planet. It's the third planet from the Sun and is the only planet in our solar system that has flowing water on its surface.

About seventy percent of the **Earth's** surface is covered with water. Mountains, volcanoes, valleys, plains and **deserts** cover the remaining thirty percent.

 **Earth** has one Moon.

Our Moon is like a very dry **desert.**

The Moon has had visitors! It is the only place in our solar system where humans have gone. In 1969 the Apollo 11 spaceship carried astronauts Neil Armstrong and Edwin "Buzz" Aldrin to the Moon to explore its surface. Neil Armstrong was the first person to walk on the Moon.

He left his footprints there.

There is no air there to blow them away.

His footprints are still there!

Astronauts go through years of specialized training. They must have strong skills in science, math, and technology.

The **astronauts** that go into space must learn how to function in weightless environments and even learn how to do a space walk.

Sometimes **astronauts** train under water. The water helps them know what it might feel like to float in space.

 Astronauts must have special **clothing,** food, and equipment to go into space.

During launch and re-entry they wear a special suit that has a helmet, gloves, and boots to protect them from changes in pressure when they leave and return from space.

Once they are in space, they can wear the same kind of **clothing** they might wear at home.

To make it easier to carry food into space, some of the food is freeze dried—a special process used to remove all of the water from the food. Before astronauts eat their freeze-dried food, they put the water back in it.

Their drinks are carried in pouches, similar to the drink pouches some kids carry in their lunch boxes.

Space food

 Astronauts like to try out their food
before they go into space.
Some astronauts like to eat hot dogs.
Some like to eat ice cream and cake!

Some astronauts must learn how to pilot the **Space Shuttle.**

The **Space Shuttle** is like an airplane, a rocket, and a spaceship all in one! It takes off like a rocket, circles the Earth like a spaceship, and lands like an airplane.

Astronauts work and sleep on the **Space Shuttle.**

Sometimes they sleep in sleeping bags.

They are tied to the wall so they won't float away.

A special spacesuit is needed when astronauts leave their spaceship while in orbit. The spacesuit is called an "extravehicular mobility unit", or EMU.

The EMU controls and monitors the astronaut's body temperature and breathing. It has a headphone and microphone so the astronaut can communicate with the Shuttle.

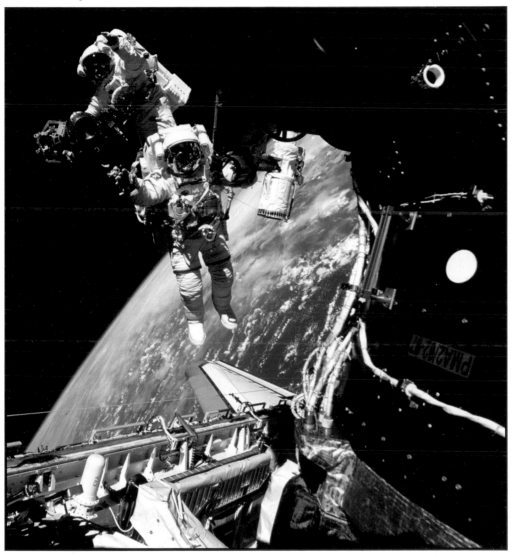

 Astronauts may also leave the
ship wearing a special backpack.
This backpack lets them move
freely through space.

How would you like to *live* in space? Some astronauts do. There are teams of astronauts that take turns living and working on space stations.

Space stations are enormous satellites that orbit the Earth.

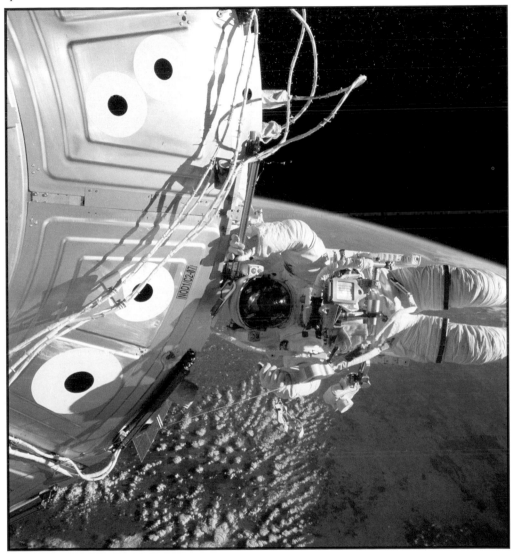

 Space stations are made up of many different parts.
Astronauts put these parts together in space.

There have been two famous space stations in the past, the United States Skylab, and the Russian Mir.

The biggest space station ever is the International Space Station.

 Astronauts from many different places live on this space station. They work together to learn more about space.

There is so much more **exciting** information to learn about space. Maybe someday you will be a scientist or an astronomer. Perhaps you will make new discoveries and explore distant galaxies.

What if you were an astronaut?

Think of all the **exciting** things you could do.

Maybe you could be the first person to walk

on Mars!

If you liked
About Space, here are two other
We Both Read® Books you are sure to enjoy!

The oceans come alive in this new non-fiction title in the *We Both Read* series. Filled with beautiful photographs, this book explores many aspects of the ocean environment that will excite readers, both young and old! Journey from coral reefs to deep seas to sandy shores. Learn interesting facts about life in the ocean, including dolphins, sharks, whales, starfish and much more!

To see all the We Both Read books that are available,
just go online to **www.webothread.com**

Explore the mystery and wonder of the tropical rain forest! Travel around the equator to Africa, Asia, and South America discovering the world's most fascinating plant and animal life. Captivating photographs, along with compelling text, make this Level 1–2 book an exciting adventure and a great learning experience.